Seeds to 🌳 Trees

Faithfulness in the Bible

Written by:
Sunny Kang

Illustrated by:
Alexandro Ockyno

Text and Illustrations Copyright © 2021 Sunny Kang
All rights reserved. No part of this publication may be reproduced, distributed, or transmitted in any form or by any means, including photocopying, recording, or other electronic or mechanical methods, without the prior written permission of the publisher, except in the case of brief quotations embodied in reviews and certain other non-commercial uses permitted by copyright law.
The moral right of the author and illustrator has been asserted.
Cover design and illustrations by Alexandro Ockyno

E-Book: 978-1-7363548-6-5
Paperback: 978-1-7363548-7-2
Hardcover: 978-1-7363548-8-9

May you always walk by FAITH and not by sight!

—2 Corinthians 5:7—

To :

From :

Date :

What is Faithfulness?

Faithfulness is being good
or trustworthy,
over a long period of time.

Adam

And God saw everything that he had made,
and behold it was very good.
- Genesis 1:31 -

In the beginning, God created everything.
He made the earth and even the entire universe.
He made the skies, waters, and lands.
Then He filled the skies with birds, the waters with fish,
and the lands with plants and animals.

Adam and Eve lived in the Garden of Eden.
God said they could eat from any tree in the Garden,
except from the Tree of Knowledge,
or else there would be big trouble.

Noah

Noah was a righteous man, blameless in his generation.
Noah walked with God.
– Genesis 6:9 –

Many years after Adam and Eve, people began to multiply and fill the world. Most people did not do what was right in God's eyes. They knew God's ways, but did not follow Him.

But Noah was a righteous man with a wife and three sons, who were each married.

One day,
God called Noah to build an enormous ark.
He was going to send a huge flood to the world
to begin again with Noah and his family.

After the ark was built,
Noah and his family went in the ark along
with two of every land animal
and flying creature.

Also included were seven pairs
of clean animals for offerings.
God closed the door of the ark and it rained heavily
for forty days and nights.

Abraham

And I will make of you [Abraham] a great nation,
and I will bless you and make your name great,
so that you will be a blessing.

– Genesis 12:2 –

Abram was a man from the land of Ur. He had a wife, Sarai, and a nephew named Lot.

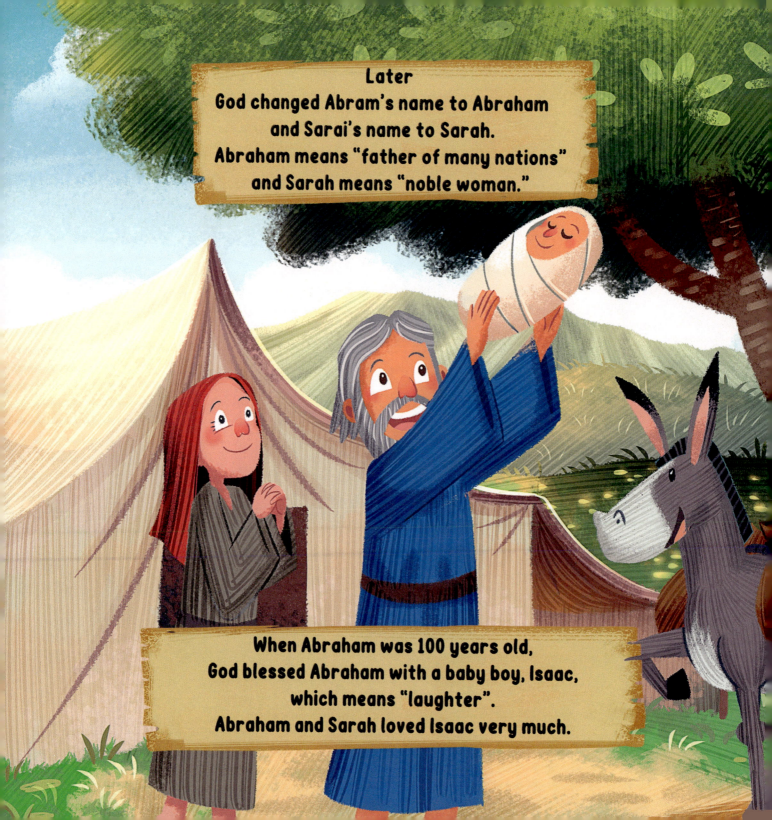

Later
God changed Abram's name to Abraham
and Sarai's name to Sarah.
Abraham means "father of many nations"
and Sarah means "noble woman."

When Abraham was 100 years old,
God blessed Abraham with a baby boy, Isaac,
which means "laughter".
Abraham and Sarah loved Isaac very much.

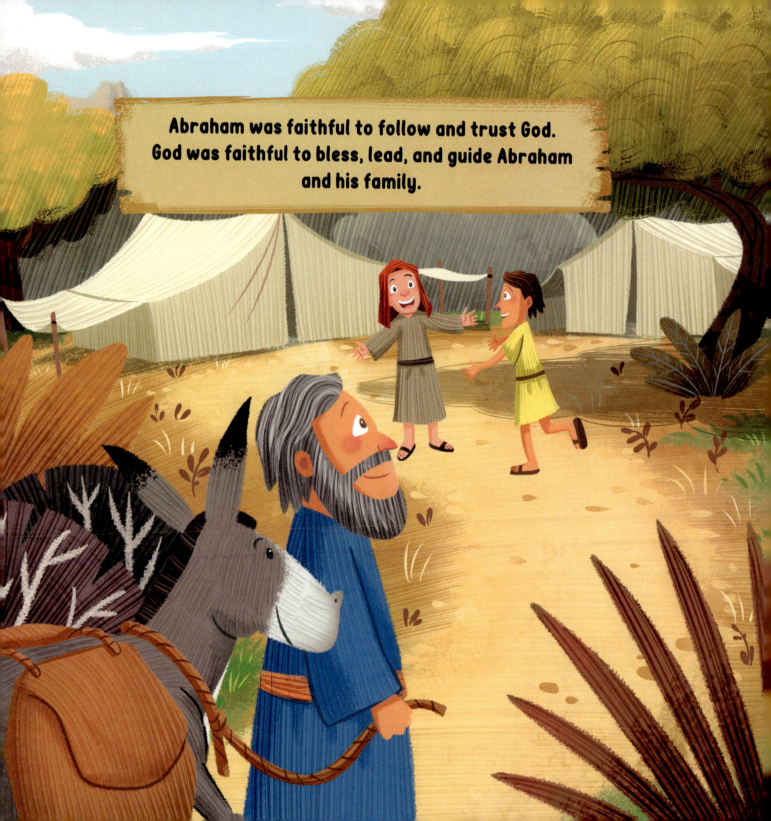

Abraham was faithful to follow and trust God. God was faithful to bless, lead, and guide Abraham and his family.

Jacob

So Jacob served seven years for Rachel, and they seemed to him but a few days because of the love he had for her.

– Genesis 29:20 –

One day Isaac married Rebekah. They had Jacob and Esau, who were twins. When the twins were born, Jacob was grabbing the heel of his brother who came out first.

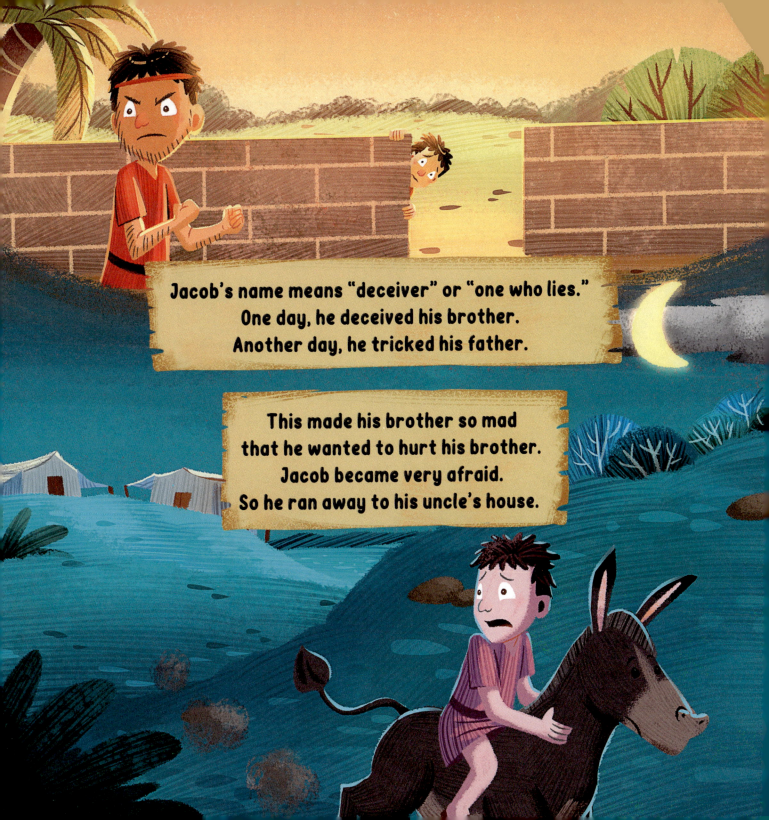

Jacob's name means "deceiver" or "one who lies."
One day, he deceived his brother.
Another day, he tricked his father.

This made his brother so mad
that he wanted to hurt his brother.
Jacob became very afraid.
So he ran away to his uncle's house.

Jacob was now far from his mother and father.
He lived with his Uncle Laban for fourteen years.
They were hard years.
After Jacob agreed to work for Uncle Laban for seven years,
his uncle tricked him to work for another seven years!

After leaving Uncle Laban's house, God changed Jacob's name to Israel, which means "one who overcomes." Jacob was now free from Uncle Laban and even made peace with his brother, Esau!

In the end, Jacob had twelve sons and one daughter. Jacob was faithful to work hard for Uncle Laban for fourteen years. God was faithful to guide and bless Jacob.

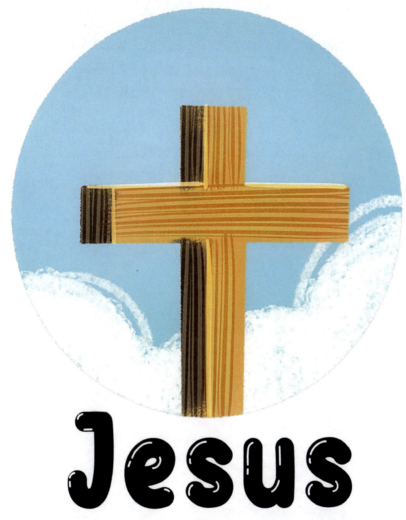

Jesus

For God so loved the world, that he gave his only Son, that whoever believes in him should not perish but have eternal life.

− John 3:16 −

When Jesus was twelve years old, his family traveled to Jerusalem to celebrate the Passover. Afterwards, his family traveled to go back home, but they forgot Jesus!

After three days, they found Jesus teaching the teachers in the temple. Then Mary remembered God was Jesus' heavenly father.

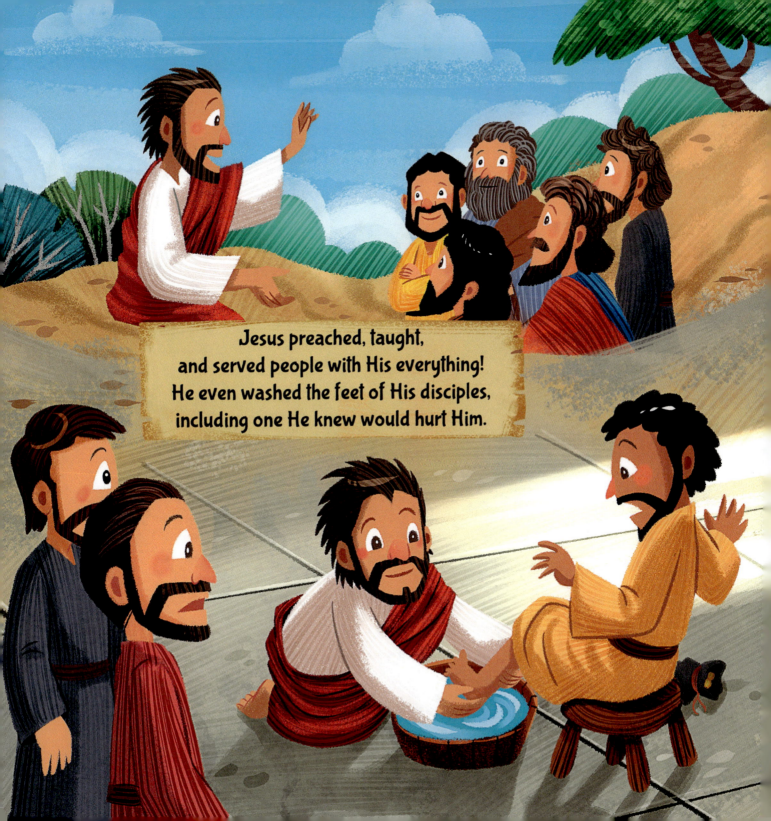

Jesus was faithful to show what God is like to people.
He loved them. He served them.
The greatest love He showed His people was
when He died on the cross.
Jesus was faithful to the very end and is even faithful now!

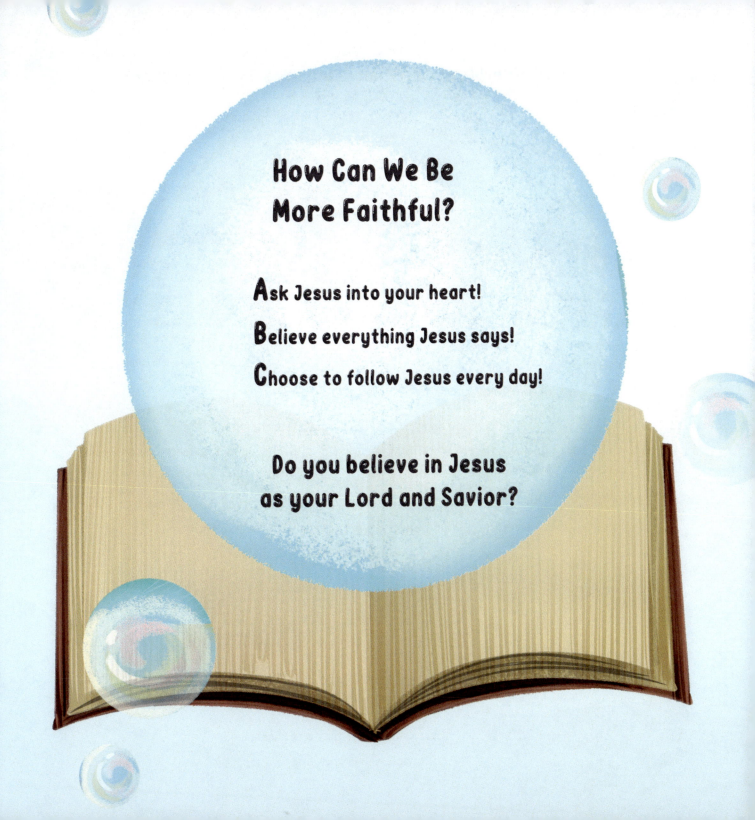

How Can We Be More Faithful?

Ask Jesus into your heart!

Believe everything Jesus says!

Choose to follow Jesus every day!

Do you believe in Jesus as your Lord and Savior?

About CornerStone Christian Academy & Tykes Preschool

Ms. Amy Benson,
Tykes Pre-School
Director

CornerStone Christian Academy & Tykes Preschool exists to encourage the development of the whole child engaging the student's spiritual, academic, and physical growth. It is our desire as followers of Christ, to pursue excellence in all that we do.

Our curriculum centers on Christ, Social & Emotional Learning, and age appropriate subject matters. The book you hold in your hands is an example of the biblical values we teach our students.

For More Information:
Website: www.ccanv.com
Instagram: @cornerstone_lv
Facebook: @lvcornerstone2

About the Author and Illustrator

Author
Sunny Kang is a Christ follower, husband, father, teacher, preacher, and author. He has pastored for over 10 years, serving as children's pastor for several of those years. He enjoys learning, meeting new people, communicating God's Word, superhero movies, and boba! He, his wife, and 2 sons live and serve in Las Vegas.

Follow Author:
Facebook: @AuthorSunnyKang
Instagram: @AuthorSunnyKang
Newsletter: http://bit.ly/authorsunnykang

Illustrator
Alexandro Ockyno is a full time freelance illustrator, living in Bali for almost 9 years. A happy man with a beautiful girlfriend, his dream is to create many children's books and share God's blessings with many others.

Follow Illustrator:
Facebook: @alessandro.altobelly
Instagram: @catandsashimi

Thank you
and hope you enjoyed this 1ˢᵗ book
in the "Seeds to Trees" series!

DOWNLOAD YOUR FREE GIFT HERE!

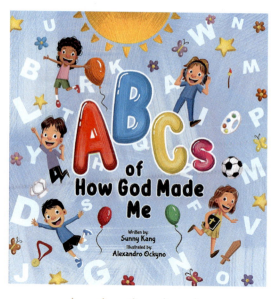

Link: https://bit.ly/ABCs-How-God-Made-Me

Made in the USA
Middletown, DE
15 October 2021